Parrots

by Helen Frost

red macaw

Consulting Editor: Gail Saunders-Smith, Ph.D.

Consultant: Alejandro Grajal, Ph.D.
Executive Director, Latin America Programs
National Audubon Society

Pebble Books

an imprint of Capstone Press
Mankato, Minnesota

Pebble Books are published by Capstone Press
151 Good Counsel Drive, P.O. Box 669, Mankato, Minnesota 56002
http://www.capstone-press.com

1 2 3 4 5 6 07 06 05 04 03 02

Library of Congress Cataloging-in-Publication Data
Frost, Helen, 1949–
    Parrots/by Helen Frost.
    p. cm.—(Rain forest animals)
    Includes bibliographical references (p. 23) and index.
    Summary: Simple text and photographs from the rain forest present the
characteristics and behavior of parrots.
    ISBN 0-7368-1194-X
    1. Parrots—Juvenile literature. [1. Parrots.] I. Title. II. Series.
QL696.P7 F76 2002
598.7′1—dc21   2001003085

Note to Parents and Teachers

The Rain Forest Animals series supports national science standards
related to life science. This book describes and illustrates parrots
that live in the rain forest. The photographs support early readers
in understanding the text. The repetition of words and phrases
helps early readers learn new words. This book also introduces
early readers to subject-specific vocabulary words, which are
defined in the Words to Know section. Early readers may need
assistance to read some words and to use the Table of Contents,
Words to Know, Read More, Internet Sites, and Index/Word List
sections of the book.

Table of Contents

Parrots are birds.
Birds have wings
and feathers.

St. Vincent Amazon parrot

African gray parrot

scarlet macaw

6

Some parrots
are white or gray.
Other parrots
are many colors.

Parrots have strong
feet. Their feet have
two toes in front
and two toes in back.

mealy parrot

Parrots have a strong beak that is shaped like a hook.

red lored Amazon parrot

places parrots live

Parrots live in
tropical rain forests.

emergent layer

canopy layer

understory layer

forest floor

14

Parrots fly through the canopy layer of the rain forest.

Parrots eat fruits,
flowers, seeds, and nuts.

hyacinth macaw

Some parrots
live together in flocks.
They build nests in trees.

hyacinth macaws

Parrots fly among
the trees during the
day. They sleep
on branches at night.

blue and yellow macaws

Words to Know

beak—the hard part of a bird's mouth; parrots have a strong beak to help them crack nuts and eat fruit.

canopy—the layer of treetops that forms a covering over a rain forest; parrots live in the canopy.

feather—one of the light, fluffy parts that cover a bird's body; parrot feathers are many colors.

flock—a group of the same kind of animal; members of flocks live, travel, and eat together.

nest—a place birds build to lay their eggs and raise their young; parrots often build their nests in the canopy.

tropical rain forest—a dense area of trees where rain falls almost every day

Read More

Altman, Linda Jacobs. *Parrots.* Perfect Pets. New York: Benchmark Books, 2001.

Kalman, Bobbie. *Rainforest Birds.* Birds up Close. New York: Crabtree Publishing, 1998.

Rauzon, Mark J. *Parrots around the World.* Animals in Order. New York: Franklin Watts, 2001.

Internet Sites

Rain Forest Animals
http://www.abcteach.com/rainforestFacts/rainforest animals3.htm

Scarlet Macaw
http://www.enchantedlearning.com/subjects/birds/printouts/scarletmacaw.shtml

Tropical Rainforest Animals
http://www.ran.org/kids_action/s2_animals.html

Index/Word List

back, 9
beak, 11
birds, 5
branches, 21
build, 19
canopy layer, 15
colors, 7
day, 21
eat, 17
feathers, 5

feet, 9
flocks, 19
flowers, 17
fly, 15, 21
front, 9
fruits, 17
hook, 11
live, 13, 19
nests, 19
night, 21

nuts, 17
rain forest, 13, 15
seeds, 17
sleep, 21
strong, 9, 11
toes, 9
together, 19
trees, 19, 21
wings, 5

Word Count: 94
Early-Intervention Level: 12

Editorial Credits

Sarah Lynn Schuette, editor; Jennifer Schonborn, production designer and interior illustrator; Linda Clavel and Heidi Meyer, cover designers; Kia Bielke, interior illustrator; Kimberly Danger and Mary Englar, photo researchers

Photo Credits

Bruce Coleman, Inc., 4, 6 (top), 18, 20
Byron Jorjorian, 10
Corel, 1
Digital Vision, 12 (background)
Rob and Ann Simpson, 8
Tom and Pat Leeson, cover, 6 (bottom)
Visuals Unlimited/Henry Lehn, 16

The author thanks the children's section staff at the Allen County Public Library in Fort Wayne, Indiana, for research assistance.